Pray That You May *Escape*
Study Guide
Second Edition

Pray That You May *Escape*
Study Guide
Second Edition

An Eye-Opening Look at the World around You

By Jeffrey R. Camino

Pray That You May Escape Study Guide
Second Edition
Copyright © 2010 Jeffrey R. Camino

All rights reserved. No part of this book may be reproduced in any form or by any electronic or mechanical means including information storage and retrieval systems, without permission in writing from the author. The only exception is by a reviewer, who may quote short excerpts in a review.

Published in Manhattan, KS
by NorthStar Solutions, LLC
1228 Westloop Pl, Suite 204
Manhattan, KS 66502

Printed in the United States of America

Unless otherwise noted, Scripture quotations are taken from the HOLY BIBLE, NEW INTERNATIONAL VERSION®. Copyright © 1973, 1978, 1984 Biblica. Used by permission of Zondervan. All rights reserved.

ISBN: 1453817360

www.LearnBibleProphecy.com

Contents

Introduction 1
Chapter 1 Bible Prophecy: Relevant for Today 5
Chapter 2 The Nation of Israel in Prophecy 9
Chapter 3 An Overview of Major End-Times Events 15
Chapter 4 Natural Disasters and Signs from Heaven 21
Chapter 5 The Moral Decay of Society 25
Chapter 6 Increase of Apostasy in the Church 29
Chapter 7 Current World Politics and Bible Prophecy 35
Chapter 8 The United States' Role in End-Times Prophecy ... 39
Chapter 9 Technology Enables End-Times Events 43
Chapter 10 Signs to Watch For 47
Chapter 11 Further Study 53
Chapter 12 What to Do Now .... .57
Related Bible Verses 61

INTRODUCTION

I am excited that you chose to study Bible prophecy more in depth—and I am especially honored that you chose this study guide to help you do so. I've received many comments from readers of *Pray That You May Escape* letting me know how thankful they were to come across a book about end times Bible prophecy that is especially easy to understand and yet still provides a substantial amount of information about the topic. I pray that, coupled with the book, this study guide will help you understand the fascinating topic of Bible prophecy even more.

Another impression I often get from readers is that they desire to share what they learned with others, which is another reason this study guide exists. Like many of you and other leading eschatologists of our time, I am convinced that we are living near the end times, and that means that it's more important than ever that God's prophetic Word be shared! Indeed the Bible tells us that the Lord gave us prophecy so that we can understand His plans:

> *Surely the Sovereign LORD does nothing without revealing his plan to his servants the prophets.* (Amos 3:7)

You will find this study guide equally helpful whether you plan to do a personal study to deepen your understanding of the topic or you plan to explore the subject within a study group. Regardless of which setting you are in, once you complete the lessons, you will be better able to defend your positions concerning God's Word about what will happen in the end days. It will also help when opportunities to evangelize non-

Christians are provided to you, as you will be able to confidently point to God's prophetic Word in light of recent history and current events. Moreover, you will find yourself better equipped to challenge fellow Christians that need a stronger relationship with Christ given that now, more than ever, is not a time to be sitting on the proverbial fence in our Christian walk. Jesus tells us in Revelation 3:17 that He will reject a "lukewarm" church, "So, because you are lukewarm—neither hot nor cold—I am about to spit you out of my mouth."

One section of this study guide you may also find useful is the one at the back of the book, where I have included over 100 Bible verses that can be found in *Pray That You May Escape*. I hope that you will find that helpful for quickly locating a verse you are familiar with, but do not know exactly where it may be found in the Bible and/or to help you become more familiar with some especially important prophecy-related verses.

One of the things I learned to appreciate during my career as a professional software developer is that great software is always designed to be as easy to use as possible. Thus, it does not have a lot of "fluff" and/or extraneous options that lends to making the product cumbersome and unfriendly. Along that train of thought, this study guide has also been intentionally kept lightweight: without a lot of extra text or stories that often just cloud the topic and make a book more weighty than necessary.

You will get the most benefit from this study guide if you first read the corresponding chapter in the book (either for the first time or as a refresher) and then answer each question. The questions in this study guide have been carefully selected to highlight each chapter/topic so that you will better learn the main points, to make you think deeper, and to stimulate conversation in a small group setting.

If you are studying the material in a small group, you will find that most chapters provide a substantial amount of material for discussion. There are, however, a couple of chapters that may go by relatively quickly. Chapter one will likely be one of them, but typically the first night of a study group is used to introduce the material and perhaps even get acquainted with one another. As for the other couple of "light" chapters, rather than "pad" them with extra questions in order to make them artificially longer, I hope that you will use any extra time to fellowship and to discuss prophecy-related news. The following web page will provide you with some help as you explore today's headlines:

http://www.LearnBibleProphecy.com/news

Regardless of if you are using this study guide alone or in a group setting, if you come across a question that you would like answered or clarified (or if you just want to discuss something more), feel free to contact me at:

http://www.LearnBibleProphecy.com/contact

Many Blessings,

Jeffrey R. Camino
Jeffrey R. Camino, Author
Pray That You May Escape

CHAPTER 1

BIBLE PROPHECY: RELEVANT FOR TODAY

Although many Christians often miss how often the Bible discusses prophecy, people that study the topic know that God put a lot of emphasis on prophecy. Consequently it is a subject that definitely should be studied. It is, therefore, important that those of us that understand that important concept try to introduce the topic to others. What happens is much like what happens with the Parable of the Sower (Matthew 13:1-23, Mark 4:1-20, and Luke 8:4-15): at times it will fall in places (along the path, on rock, or amongst thorns) and not yield anything; at other times, however, it will fall on fertile ground and produce a fantastic crop. I trust because you have chosen this study guide, you are providing a fertile ground for God's Word to grow and multiply.

In fact, as noted in *Pray That You May Escape*, over 20 percent of the New Testament contains prophecy and a total of 27 percent of the entire Bible is prophecy related. Prophecy has many purposes: it can be used to help provide validation that Jesus is the Messiah, and it gives Christians living near or in the end times a blueprint for God's plans.

Until recently, end-times prophecy was not that well understood; but due to recent historical events we are beginning to understand Bible prophecy more than ever. That important concept contributes to the fact that many Bible scholars believe we are now living in the end times because God explained that our knowledge of prophecy would substantially increase at "the time of the end" (Daniel 12:9).

1. Most people know that the Book of Revelations contains a lot of prophecy; however, it is not the only book in the Bible where the Lord chose to provide prophetic insights into future events. List some other books of the Bible where end-times prophecy is discussed.

2. The Bible has several verses that specifically explain why Bible prophecy is important to study. What is one of your favorites and why?

3. Daniel wrote, "I heard, but I did not understand. So I asked, 'My lord, what will the outcome of all this be?' He replied, 'Go your way, Daniel, because the words are closed up and sealed until the time of the end'" (Daniel 12:8-9). Why are those words important to us today?

4. What was your initial reaction to the idea of studying Bible prophecy? How do you feel about studying the topic now?

5. It is important that Christians understand Bible prophecy if they are open to doing so. What are some ways you can introduce the topic to others?

6. We know that according to 2 Peter 3:2-4 some people will scoff when end times Bible prophecy is mentioned. Do you believe the words of Jesus in Luke 9:5 could be similarly applied to situations where we present information about end times Bible prophecy to people and they do not want to hear it?

CHAPTER 2

THE NATION OF ISRAEL IN PROPHECY

The Bible makes it clear that we should continue to watch the nation of Israel because God has chosen Israel for special purposes, both historically and for the fulfillment of end-times prophecy. Israel is getting a lot of attention in news headlines these days. When one studies the history of Israel and lines that up with God's Word, the results (at least for Christians) are very exciting. Jesus assured us when He spoke to some of His disciple on the Mount of Olives that once end-time events started, they would not last over a prolonged time.

> *"However, the days are coming," declares the Lord, "when men will no longer say, 'As surely as the Lord lives, who brought the Israelites up out of Egypt,' but they will say, 'As surely as the Lord lives, who brought the Israelites up out of the land of the north and out of all the countries where he had banished them.' For I will restore them to the land I gave their forefathers".* (Jeremiah 16:14-15)

5-14-1948

1. How are those words found in Jeremiah relevant to us today?

_____

_____

_____

_____

_____

2. On May 14, 1948 Israel became a nation once again. Explain why, relative to church history, that important prophetic event was not that long ago?

3. Many people believe the Jewish people are occupying Israel illegally and have no right to the land. What does the Bible have to say about that in Genesis 15:18-21? Does God's promise indicate any conditions or time limit?

4. Typically when a group of people are absorbed into the political, economic, and social systems of other lands, they lose their identity, customs, and religious practices. Did that happen to the Jewish people?

5. The Six Day war of 1967 was miraculous because Israel defeated its enemy despite being significantly outnumbered. This enabled Israel to recapture Jerusalem. How is it prophetically important that the Jews control Jerusalem?

6. While speaking to His disciples on the Mount of Olives, Jesus said, "Now learn this lesson from the fig tree: As soon as its twigs get tender and its leaves come out, you know that summer is near. Even so, when you see all these things, you know that it is near, right at the door. I tell you the truth, this generation will certainly not pass away until all these things have happened." (Matthew 24:32). Discuss why many eschatologists believe that is very important to us today.

7. According to Psalm 90:10, what is the definition of a generation?

8. Have the Jewish people been forgotten by God? What scriptural evidence do you have to support your answer?

9. Returning to the discussion of the fig tree, some critics ask, "If the fig tree is truly representing Israel, then why did Luke also mention other trees?" Do you agree with that response or is there some other explanation about why Matthew did not include "and all the trees" as Luke did?

10. What does the Apostle Paul write in Romans 11:25 about the Jews' hearts? Why is that important to Christians? Does it suggest that some day the Jews will turn to God again and accept Christ as their Messiah?

Blood Moon - Jewish Holidays

Matt 24
Mark 13
Luke 21

Romans 9-10-11

CHAPTER 3

AN OVERVIEW OF END-TIMES EVENTS

*F*or the Lord himself will come down from heaven, with a loud command, with the voice of the archangel and with the trumpet call of God, and the dead in Christ will rise first. After that, we who are <u>still alive and are left will be caught up</u> together with them in the clouds to meet the Lord in the air. And so we will be with the Lord forever. (1 Thessalonians 4:16-18) *2nd 2:13 1 Cor 15:50-58 Lk 17:26-36*

Rev. 4:18 2ND coming Matt

1. The Rapture is often confused with the Second Coming of Christ. What are some of the attributes of each that clearly distinguish one from the other?

....

....

....

....

....

....

2. Probably the single most debated topic in eschatology is the timing of the Rapture. Is it a matter of salvation? Why is the issue so often debated and what is the proper way Christians should discuss the topic?

3. What are the four main theories about the timing of the Rapture?

4. The author of *Pray That You May Escape* agrees with the Pre-Tribulation Rapture Theory. Do you agree with it? Why or why not?

_____

_____

_____

_____

_____

_____

5. In Luke 21:36, Jesus says, "Pray that you may be able to escape all that is about to happen". Why is the word "all" important?

_____

_____

_____

_____

18 / *Pray That You May Escape*

6. Read Luke 17:20-37, and continue to Luke 18:1-8. What do you notice about the transition between those two chapters? Is the same topic being discussed?

7. In Luke 17:20-37, Jesus provides an account of events that describe the Rapture (two people are working, one disappears; two people are in bed, one is taken). What are some of the activities being described when He says it will be like those that happened during the days of Noah? Do they appear to be during the tribulation or prior to the tribulation? Why?

8. Why is knowing the concept of Daniel's 70th Week so important to understanding end-times prophecy?

9. "Tribulation Saints" is a term eschatologists give to the people that will be left behind after the Rapture, and then later confess Jesus as their Lord and Savior. Why is it important that we recognize that Tribulation Saints will exist in the last days?

10. Although we are obviously given many signs to look for as signs of the end times, Jesus discusses if we will know the *exact* timing of the Rapture many times in His Olivet Discourse. What is the resounding theme of that discussion?

11. In 2 Peter 3:2-4 we read how many people will react when end times Bible prophecy is discussed. What is that reaction? Does it describe many peoples' reactions today?

12. The study of Bible prophecy is obviously very important and arguably more important now than it has ever been. As Christians we should always look for opportunities to witness to others and to encourage one another. How can we look for such opportunities and how do we help people understand the importance of Bible prophecy?

CHAPTER 4

NATURAL DISASTERS AND SIGNS FROM HEAVEN

"There will be great earthquakes, famines and pestilences in various places, and fearful events and great signs from heaven" (Luke 21:11).

1. Earthquakes seem to be the one natural disaster Christians and non-Christians alike know the Bible warns us about relative to the end times. As noted in the verse above, there are other signs to watch for too. Do they seem like they could be related to one another?

2. When you hear that earthquakes and other natural disasters seem to be increasing, how do you react? How do you think we should present the fact the Bible says earthquakes, tsunamis, famines, and pestilence (among other things) will increase in the end days?

3. When Jesus explains that end-times events will occur like "birth pains", what does that mean?

4. If birth pains do not substantially increase until just before a baby is born, what does that tell us about how the intensity of end-times natural disasters will happen?

5. It seems that the more we learn from science, the more we realize how much we don't know. How do you think that concept could affect end-times events?

6. Does it seem possible that some events related to the natural disasters or signs in the heavens described to happen in the end times could happen prior to the actual event (some warnings, so to speak)? What types of events does *Pray That You May Escape* suggest could lead to cosmic events "like which have not been seen before"?

7. As Christians, how much should we rely on science to understand prophecy given we know God has the ability to do things outside the realm of what we understand? Should we also be aware of science, the world in which we live, and news related to that? What do you think is the best approach to that?

CHAPTER 5

THE MORAL DECAY OF SOCIETY

But mark this: There will be terrible times in the last days. People will be lovers of themselves, lovers of money, boastful, proud, abusive, disobedient to their parents, ungrateful, unholy, without love, unforgiving, slanderous, without self-control, brutal, not lovers of the good, treacherous, rash, conceited, lovers of pleasure rather than lovers of God. (2 Timothy 3:1-4)

1. What are some of the attributes that people will have in the end days according to 2 Timothy 3:1-4. Does that seem to be descriptive of society today?

2. Briefly contrast some of the problems school teachers and administrators experienced a few decades ago with the problems that are being faced by them today.

3. How does the entertainment industry reflect the moral decay of society? Do you think Christians should watch the same type of entertainment that non-Christians do? Why or why not?

4. List some of the places in the Bible that discuss homosexuality and summarize what God's Word says about it.

5. How should Christians react to homosexuality? How should Christians react to homosexuals?

6. We know that the moral decay of society will happen because it is foretold to happen in the Bible. As Christians we are also told not to conform to the pattern of this world (Romans 12:2). How, then, do we live in this world, but not take part in the moral depravity?

CHAPTER 6

INCREASE OF APOSTASY IN THE CHURCH

At that time many will turn away from the faith and will betray and hate each other, and many false prophets will appear and deceive many people. (Matthew 24:10-11)

For the time will come when men will not put up with sound doctrine. Instead, to suit their own desires, they will gather around them a great number of teachers to say what their itching ears want to hear. They will turn their ears away from the truth and turn aside to myths. (2 Timothy 4:3-4)

1. Apostasy has arguably increased substantially in the past few decades. Provide examples of how we witness that today.

_____

_____

_____

_____

_____

2. What does the concept of "itching ears" referred to in 2 Timothy 4:3-4 mean?

3. How does most of society treat Christians that stand upon the Word of God and say that Jesus is the only way to heaven?

4. How does the rejection of Jesus being the only way to heaven insult God's plan of salvation?

5. Do churches that accept sinful lifestyles ultimately help or hurt the people they are accepting? Why?

6. Summarize how the church should act toward sin according to chapters two and three of Revelation.

7. According to *Pray That You May Escape*, what is one of the worst apostasies in the church today? Do you agree or disagree? Why?

8. List the acts of the sinful nature as described in Galatians 5:19-20 and the consequences of committing those acts.

9. How does John 8:11 complete John 8:7?

10. How does Romans 3:31 complete Romans 3:22?

11. Summarize what the following verses say about continually sinning: 1 John 3:7-11, Matthew 7:21-23, 1 John 3:5-6, and Titus 2:11-14

12. We know that Christians do not become perfect and sinless just because they accept Christ into their lives. Indeed James 3:2 explains that we all will stumble, and in Galatians 2:11-13 we read that Paul scolded Peter for hypocrisy. How, then, do we provide a distinction between that and what we also know the scripture says about continuing to sin?

13. What should we do when we sin?

CHAPTER 7

CURRENT WORLD POLITICS AND BIBLE PROPHECY

Many geopolitical events are happening today that suggest how Israel will be at war at any time, just as it is foretold to happen in the end days. We read in Ezekiel 38:1-6:

> *The word of the LORD came to me: "Son of man, set your face against Gog, of the land of Magog, the chief prince of Meshech and Tubal; prophesy against him and say: 'This is what the Sovereign Lord says: I am against you, O Gog, chief prince of Meshech and Tubal. I will turn you around, put hooks in your jaws and bring you out with your whole army—your horses, your horsemen fully armed, and a great horde with large and small shields, all of them brandishing their swords. Persia, Cush and Put will be with them, all with shields and helmets, also Gomer with all its troops, and Beth Togarmah from the far north with all its troops—the many nations with you.*

1. What nation fits the description "from the far north"? How are current events now suggesting that nation is poised to reemerge on the international scene?

2. Ezekiel 38 also mentions Persia. What modern day country used to be called Persia? What is the name of their current leader and what is his attitude towards Israel.

3. Prophecy experts are beginning to take a close look at Psalm 83, which describes events that could almost be pulled straight out of today's headlines. Nations that share borders with Israel continue to line up against her, lobbing missiles and instigating attacks against Israeli citizens. List some of those nations:

4. In 1 Thessalonians 5:1-9 Paul writes, "While people are saying, 'Peace and safety,' destruction will come on them suddenly, as labor pains on a pregnant woman, and they will not escape. But you, brothers, are not in darkness so that this day should surprise you like a thief." Do you believe Israel is currently living in a state of peace? Why or why not?

5. In Daniel 2:31-33, the prophet Daniel told Nebuchadnezzar, "You looked, O king, and there before you stood a large statue—an enormous, dazzling statue, awesome in appearance. The head of the statue was made of pure gold, its chest and arms of silver, its belly and thighs of bronze, its legs of iron, its feet partly of iron and partly of baked clay." What previous empires are represented in Nebuchadnezzar's dream?

38 / Pray That You May Escape

6. How is the last empire represented?

7. Regardless of what nations make the last empire that Daniel predicts, what nation do we know, without a doubt, will be part of the end times scenario?

CHAPTER 8

THE UNITED STATES' ROLE IN END-TIMES PROPHECY

In Zechariah 12:2-3, we read:

> *I am going to make Jerusalem a cup that sends all the surrounding peoples reeling. Judah will be besieged as well as Jerusalem. On that day, when all the nations of the earth are gathered against her, I will make Jerusalem an immovable rock for all the nations. All who try to move it will injure themselves.*

1. In light of what we read in the passages above, does it suggest that the United States will continue to be an ally of Israel and, as the world's current superpower, offer protection to Israel and her people?

_____

_____

_____

_____

2. Does the United States currently seem to support Israel as much as it has in the past? Why or why not?

_____

_____

3. Many eschatologists theorize that an event could occur in the end times that would cause the United States to dramatically withdrawal its support of Israel. What is that event and what are some of the reasons it would lead to that scenario?

4. The United States is currently engaged in a war on terrorism, how might that explain why the United States is not mentioned in end-times Bible prophecy?

5. The United States is currently heavily reliant on foreign oil to sustain it's economy and military, how might that explain why the United States is not mentioned in end-times Bible prophecy?

6. The United States is currently in a severe economic downturn and many experts believe it is headed into a period of unprecedented inflation. What are some of the reasons they believe that? Is that predicted to happen in the Bible? How might that explain why the United States is not mentioned in end-times Bible prophecy?

CHAPTER 9

TECHNOLOGY ENABLES END-TIMES EVENTS

Advances in technology are happening at a phenomenal pace, especially in recent decades. As someone that makes their living off of the Internet (selling books and software, and building e-commerce sites), I appreciate technology as much as anyone. Moreover, as the father of six kids, some of which are currently teenagers, I can attest to the fact technology is a vital part of our everyday lives. God knew the type of technology that would be available in the end times when He provided words and visions to the prophets. Technology can be used for good, and some of it will be a sinister tool in the hands of the False Prophet and Antichrist.

1. In the past few decades advances in communication have occurred which enable sounds and images to be transmitted worldwide virtually instantaneously. As a result of that, what prophetic events can now be achieved?

44 / Pray That You May Escape

2. We read in Revelation 13:16-17:

> *He also forced everyone, small and great, rich and poor, free and slave, to receive a mark on his right hand or on his forehead, so that no one could buy or sell unless he had the mark, which is the name of the beast or the number of his name. This calls for wisdom. If anyone has insight, let him calculate the number of the beast, for it is man's number. His number is 666.*

According to Revelation 13:16, will the mark of the Beast be required for only a select group of people?

3. What types of technology exists today that would enable the Antichrist to more easily control who may buy and sell?

4. Do you believe the mark of the Beast will be obvious or do you think that people will be "tricked" into receiving it? Why or why not?

5. What does Revelation 14:9-11 and Revelation 16:2 describe will happen to people that accept the mark of the Beast?

6. According to Revelation 20:4, what will happen to people that resist accepting the mark of the Beast?

7. Christians are commanded to evangelize, as described in Matthew 28:19-20. In the Olivet Discourse, Jesus said, "And this gospel of the kingdom will be preached in the whole world as a testimony to all nations, and then the end will come." (Matthew 24:14) What types of technology do we have today that can assist making that prophecy come true?

8. Related to the previous questions, what can and should you do to obey that command and to help fulfill prophecy?

CHAPTER 10

SIGNS TO WATCH FOR

Some end-times prophecies already have been fulfilled, others are developing, and others are yet to come. Some will not happen until the middle of the tribulation, and others will not occur until the great tribulation. Thus, given that either the Pre-Tribulation Rapture Theory most correctly describe the timing of the Rapture, Christians may only see signs that prelude some of these actual events because they will be raptured to heaven before some happen.

Surely the Sovereign LORD does nothing without revealing his plan to his servants the prophets. (Amos 3:7)

Blessed is the one who reads the words of this prophecy, and blessed are those who hear it and take to heart what is written in it. (Revelation 1:3).

1. How do the words in Amos 3:7 and Revelation 1:3 encourage you to study prophecy?

_____

_____

_____

_____

2. As discussed in "Appendix A, The Olivet Discourse Analyzed and Explained", some of Jesus' words have a prophetic foreshadow (that is, some of what He described address things that we now know happened in 70 A.D, while some are events yet to come). According to the comments on pages 135-138 of *Pray That You May Escape*, what are some of the indications that Jesus was speaking of things that would happen at a time even future to 70 A.D.?

3. What major event must happen in Jerusalem before the abomination that causes desolation occurs?

4. Do you think we could witness events that initiate the Third Temple getting rebuilt? Why or why not?

5. Paul writes in 1 Thessalonians 5:1-9, "While people are saying, 'Peace and safety,' destruction will come on them suddenly, as labor pains on a pregnant woman, and they will not escape. But you, brothers, are not in darkness so that this day should surprise you like a thief." If we, as Christians, witness Israel signing a significant peace treaty wherein people begin to say Israel is living in "peace and safety" (and, thus, we conclude the beginning of the seven year tribulation has begun), does that mean there will be no early rapture? Why or why not?

6. Jesus warned us in the Olivet Discourse that there will be wars and rumors of wars in the end days, yet wars have existed since the creation of man. Do the wars and rumors of wars in recent decades seem different than the wars of that happened hundreds or thousands of years ago? Why or why not?

7. Although the United States is presently the world's single largest superpower, Scripture does not indicate the U.S. will have a major, if any, role in end times events. Many eschatologists believe that is because it may have substantially declined economically, politically, and/or militarily in the end times. Are signs of that now possibly happening? Explain.

_____
_____
_____
_____

8. We are warned that a rise in apostasy and false teachings will be prevalent in end times (Matthew 24:10-11; 2 Timothy 3:1-4). Do you have any examples of how that is happening today?

_____
_____
_____
_____
_____

9. We are told that the end times will be marked with a continued decay of morals in society (2 Timothy 3:1-4). Does society seem to have had a substantial moral decline in recent decades?

10. Are there any news headlines happening now that support what many eschatologists believe: that we are living in the end times? (Hint: http://www.LearnBibleProphecy.com/news has a reasonably good place to start researching current Bible prophecy news).

Chapter 11

Further Study

I am aware that chances are good you have, or soon will, be looking to other sources of information related to eschatology. The good news is that there is a lot of information available. The bad news is there is a lot of information available. That is why I always remind people about what Jesus warned in Matthew 24:24

> *For false Christs and false prophets will appear and perform great signs and miracles to deceive even the elect—if that were possible.*

Notice that Jesus says even Christians could be deceived, which I believe could easily happen if they did not have proper knowledge and understanding of the end-time events described in the Bible. Also note that, at this point, it is not the just Antichrist or the false prophet that is in view; rather, there will be many who are claiming to be Christ or providing false prophecy.

1. Have you ever experienced a time when you studied a topic related to the Bible and were initially convinced the author/speaker was writing/speaking the truth, and then later realized he/she was not? Explain.

2. What are some signs that indicate someone may be a false prophet?

3. What is one important habit everyone should have to help them prevent being misled by Bible teachers?

4. What does it mean to "spiritualize" the Bible when interpreting it, and why does that practice often lead to controversy and deception?

5. How does Messianic prophecy (and now, the way in which Israel became a nation) give us clues about how we should usually interpret the Bible?

6. Daniel wrote, "But you, Daniel, close up and seal the words of the scroll until the time of the end. Many will go here and there to increase knowledge." (Daniel 12:1-4) What do those words "Many will go here and there to increase knowledge" most likely mean?

56 / *Pray That You May Escape*

7. Where is one of the first places one should look when trying to interpret symbolic language in the Bible?

8. What should we all pray for when it comes to asking the Holy Spirit to help us understand God's Word?

CHAPTER 12

WHAT TO DO NOW

I am so glad you have read *Pray That You May Escape* and then took your studies a big step further and worked through this accompanying study guide. I hope and pray that it has helped you have a better understanding of end times Bible prophecy. If you are like many people that study the subject, you likely asked yourself, "Now that I understand what is going to happen, what am I supposed to do about it?" I trust chapter 12 helped answers that question for you.

1. Did God provide prophetic insight for us so that we can change end times events? Why or why not?

_____

_____

_____

_____

2. Is it dangerous to share Bible prophecy with people for fear that the information, in the wrong hands, will be turned to do evil deeds? Why or why not?

_____

_____

3. According to the Apostle Paul's words in Thessalonians 5:1-9, what does that tell us about our knowledge of Bible prophecy? How should we, as Christians, act?

4. In addition to furthering our understanding about Bible prophecy, what are some things Christians can do?

5. How does Bible prophecy enable us to encourage non-believers?

6. How can we use Bible prophecy as a tool to reach out to other Christians and help strengthen their spiritual lives?

....

....

....

....

....

RELATED BIBLE VERSES

On the next several pages you will find well over 100 Bible verses used in *Pray That You May Escape*. They have been included in this study guide to help you become more familiar with many of the most important verses related to Bible prophecy.

The verses are divided by the same chapter titles found in *Pray That You May Escape* to make locating verses in the book much easier when/if you want to. Also, since the chapter titles reflect prophecy-related subjects, it may help you better understand the context of the verses.

When it was not practical to include the full text, such as the entire second and third chapters of Revelation, a reference to those verses is provided. For the same reason, this section does not contain the entire text of the Olivet Discourse found in Matthew 24, Mark 13, and Luke 21. Of course, many selected verses from the Olivet Discourse have been included since it contains a substantial amount of end-times prophecy and consequently is referred to throughout the book. Appendix A of *Pray That You May Escape* contains the complete text to the Olivet Discourse, with the verses of Matthew, Mark, and Luke laid out side by side with some commentary and analysis.

Of course, you are encouraged to read the verses in their full text in your own Bible. On a related note, if you are looking for a great study Bible, I can highly recommend *The Full Life Study Bible-New International Version.* The late Donald C. Stamps, author of that edition, obviously had a firm grasp of eschatology and, as a result, both the notes for selected verses and the articles sprinkled throughout that edition are very solid.

CHAPTER 1

BIBLE PROPHECY: RELEVANT FOR TODAY

Be always on the watch, and pray that you may be able to escape all that is about to happen, and that you may be able to stand before the Son of Man. (Luke 21:36, quoting Jesus)

Surely the Sovereign Lord does nothing without revealing his plan to his servants the prophets. (Amos 3:7)

None of the wicked will understand, but those who are wise will understand. (Daniel 12:10)

See, I have told you ahead of time. (Matthew 24:25, quoting Jesus)

So be on your guard; I have told you everything ahead of time. (Mark 13:23, quoting Jesus)

Do not put out the Spirit's fire; do not treat prophecies with contempt. Test everything. Hold on to the good.
(1 Thessalonians 5:19-21)

And we have the word of the prophets made more certain, and you will do well to pay attention to it, as to a light shining in a dark place, until the day dawns and the morning star rises in your hearts. (2 Peter 1:19)

Above all, you must understand that no prophecy of Scripture came about by the prophet's own interpretation. For prophecy never had its origin in the will of man, but men spoke from God as they were carried along by the Holy Spirit. (2 Peter 1:20-21)

I want you to recall the words spoken in the past by the holy prophets and the command given by our Lord and Savior through your apostles. First of all, you must understand that in the last days scoffers will come, scoffing and following their own evil desires. They will say, "Where is this 'coming' he promised?" (2 Peter 3:2-4)

Blessed is the one who reads the words of this prophecy, and blessed are those who hear it and take to heart what is written in it. (Revelation 1:3)

I heard, but I did not understand. So I asked, "My lord, what will the outcome of all this be?" He replied, "Go your way, Daniel, because the words are closed up and sealed until the time of the end." (Daniel 12:8-9)

CHAPTER 2

THE NATION OF ISRAEL IN PROPHECY

"However, the days are coming," declares the LORD, "when men will no longer say, 'As surely as the LORD lives, who brought the Israelites up out of Egypt,' but they will say, 'As surely as the LORD lives, who brought the Israelites up out of the land of the north and out of all the countries where he had banished them.' For I will restore them to the land I gave their forefathers." (Jeremiah 16:14-15)

On that day the LORD made a covenant with Abram and said, "To your descendants I give this land, from the river of Egypt to the great river, the Euphrates—the land of the Kenites, Kenizzites, Kadmonites, Hittites, Perizzites, Rephaites, Amorites, Canaanites, Girgashites and Jebusites." (Genesis 15:18-21)

"Who has ever heard of such a thing? Who has ever seen such things? Can a country be born in a day or a nation be brought forth in a moment? Yet no sooner is Zion in labor than she gives birth to her children. Do I bring to the moment of birth and not give delivery?" says the Lord. "Do I close up the womb when I bring to delivery?" says your God. "Rejoice with Jerusalem and be glad for her, all you who love her; rejoice greatly with her, all you who mourn over her." (Isaiah 66:8-10)

"So when you see standing in the holy place 'the abomination that causes desolation,' spoken of through the prophet Daniel—let the reader understand—then let those who are in Judea flee to the mountains." (Matthew 24:15-16, quoting Jesus)

"He will confirm a covenant with many for one 'seven.' In the middle of the 'seven' he will put an end to sacrifice and offering. And on a wing of the temple he will set up an abomination that causes desolation, until the end that is decreed is poured out on him." (Daniel 9:27)

"Now learn this lesson from the fig tree: As soon as its twigs get tender and its leaves come out, you know that summer is near. Even so, when you see all these things, you know that it is near, right at the door. I tell you the truth, this generation will certainly not pass away until all these things have happened." (Matthew 24:32, quoting Jesus)

The length of our days is seventy years—or eighty, if we have the strength. (Psalm 90:10)

Seeing a fig tree by the road, he went up to it but found nothing on it except leaves. Then he said to it, "May you never bear fruit again!" Immediately the tree withered. (Matthew 21:19)

Then [Jesus] told this parable: "A man planted a fig tree in his garden and came again and again to see if there was any fruit on it, but he was always disappointed. Finally, he said to his gardener, 'I've waited three years, and there hasn't been a single fig! Cut it down. It's just taking up space in the garden.' The gardener answered, 'Sir, give it one more chance. Leave it another year, and

I'll give it special attention and plenty of fertilizer. If we get figs next year, fine. If not, then you can cut it down.'" (Luke 13:6-9)

Consider therefore the kindness and sternness of God: sternness to those who fell, but kindness to you, provided that you continue in his kindness. Otherwise, you also will be cut off. And if they do not persist in unbelief, they will be grafted in, for God is able to graft them in again. After all, if you were cut out of an olive tree that is wild by nature, and contrary to nature were grafted into a cultivated olive tree, how much more readily will these, the natural branches, be grafted into their own olive tree! (Romans 11:22-25)

CHAPTER 3

AN OVERVIEW OF END-TIMES EVENTS

For the Lord himself will come down from heaven, with a loud command, with the voice of the archangel and with the trumpet call of God, and the dead in Christ will rise first. After that, we who are still alive and are left will be caught up together with them in the clouds to meet the Lord in the air. And so we will be with the Lord forever. (1 Thessalonians 4:16-18)

THE RAPTURE	THE SECOND COMING
Christians will be taken from earth and will join the Lord in the clouds. (1 Thessalonians 4:17)	Christians will return from heaven to the earth with the Lord. (Revelation 19:14)
Occurs before or early in the Tribulation. Verses addressing the specific timing of the Rapture are examined in much more detail in chapter 3 of *Pray That You May Escape*.	Occurs at the very end of the entire tribulation period. Revelation chapters 6-19

Believers will be removed or delivered from the earth. 1 Thessalonians 4:13-17; 5:9	Unbelievers will be removed as an act of judgment. Matthew 24:40-41
Will happen in an instant (in "the twinkling of an eye") 1 Corinthians 15:50-54	Will be an event that is visible to everyone. Revelation 1:7 Matthew 24:29-30
Is imminent Titus 2:13 1 Thessalonians 4:13-18 1 Corinthians 15:50-54 Luke 17:26-36	Will not occur until after certain other end-times events take place. 2 Thessalonians 2:4 Matthew 24:15-30 Revelation chapters 6–18

Then Jesus told His disciples a parable to show them that they should always pray and not give up. He said, "In a certain town there was a judge who neither feared God nor cared about men. And there was a widow in that town who kept coming to him with the plea, 'Grant me justice against my adversary.' "For some time he refused. But finally he said to himself, 'Even though I don't fear God or care about men, yet because this widow keeps bothering me, I will see that she gets justice, so that she won't eventually wear me out with her coming!'" And the Lord said, "Listen to what the unjust judge says. And will not God bring about justice for his chosen ones, who cry out to him day and night? Will he keep putting them off? I tell you, he will see that they get justice, and quickly. However, when the Son of Man comes, will he find faith on the earth?" (Luke 18:1-8)

"Seventy 'sevens' are decreed for your people and your holy city to finish transgression, to put an end to sin, to atone for wickedness, to bring in everlasting righteousness, to seal up vision and prophecy and to anoint the most holy.

"Know and understand this: From the issuing of the decree to restore and rebuild Jerusalem until the Anointed One, the ruler, comes, there will be seven 'sevens,' and sixty-two 'sevens.' It will be rebuilt with streets and a trench, but in times of trouble. After the sixty-two 'sevens,' the Anointed One will be cut off and will have nothing. The people of the ruler who will come will destroy the city and the sanctuary. The end will come like a flood: War will continue until the end, and desolations have been decreed. He will confirm a covenant with many for one 'seven.' In the middle of the 'seven' he will put an end to sacrifice and offering. And on a wing of the temple he will set up an abomination that causes desolation, until the end that is decreed is poured out on him. (Daniel 9:24-27)

Then I heard the number of those who were sealed: 144,000 from all the tribes of Israel. (Revelation 7:4)

Now when they have finished their testimony, the beast that comes up from the Abyss will attack them, and overpower and kill them. Their bodies will lie in the street of the great city, which is figuratively called Sodom and Egypt, where also their Lord was crucified. For three and a half days men from every people, tribe, language and nation will gaze on their bodies and refuse them burial. The inhabitants of the earth will gloat over them and will celebrate by sending each other gifts, because these two prophets had tormented those who live on the earth. (Revelation 11:7-10)

Since you have kept my command to endure patiently, I will also keep you from the hour of trial that is going to come upon the whole world to test those who live on the earth. (Revelation 3:10, quoting Jesus)

No one knows about that day or hour, not even the angels in heaven, nor the Son, but only the Father. (Matthew 24:36, quoting Jesus)

Therefore keep watch, because you do not know on what day your Lord will come. (Matthew 24:42, quoting Jesus)

So you also must be ready, because the Son of Man will come at an hour when you do not expect him. (Matthew 24:44, quoting Jesus)

Watch therefore, for you know neither the day nor the hour in which the Son of Man is coming. (Matthew 25:13, quoting Jesus)

I want you to recall the words spoken in the past by the holy prophets and the command given by our Lord and Savior through your apostles. First of all, you must understand that in the last days scoffers will come, scoffing and following their own evil desires. They will say, "Where is this 'coming' he promised?" (2 Peter 3:2-4)

"Just as it was in the days of Noah, so also will it be in the days of the Son of Man. People were eating, drinking, marrying and being given in marriage up to the day Noah entered the ark. Then the flood came and destroyed them all. It was the same in the days of Lot. People were eating and drinking, buying and selling, planting and building. But the day Lot left Sodom, fire and sulfur rained down from heaven and destroyed them all. It will be just like this on the day the Son of Man is revealed. On that day no one who is on the roof of his house, with his goods inside, should go down to get them. Likewise, no one in the field should go back for anything. Remember Lot's wife! Whoever tries to keep his life will lose it, and whoever loses his life will preserve it. I tell you, on that night two people will be in one bed; one will be taken and the other left. Two women will be grinding grain together; one will be taken and the other left. Two men will be in a field; one taken, the other left." (Luke 17:26-36, quoting Jesus)

The Seven Seals (Revelation 6:1-17; 8:1-5)

The Seven Trumpets (Revelation 8:6-21; 11:15-19)

The Seven Bowls (Revelation 16:1-21)

Men will faint from terror, apprehensive of what is coming on the world. (Luke 21:26, quoting Jesus)

Then the kings of the earth, the princes, the generals, the rich, the mighty, and every slave and every free man hid in caves and among the rocks of the mountains. (Revelation 6:15)

For God did not appoint us to suffer wrath but to receive salvation through our Lord Jesus Christ. (1 Thessalonians 5:9)

For the secret power of lawlessness is already at work; but the one who now holds it back will continue to do so till he is taken out of the way. (2 Thessalonians 2:7)

For then there will be great tribulation, such as has not been from the beginning of the world until now, no, and never will be. (Matthew 24:21, ESV, quoting Jesus)

The coming of the lawless one will be in accordance with the work of Satan displayed in all kinds of counterfeit miracles, signs and wonders, and in every sort of evil that deceives those who are perishing. They perish because they refused to love the truth and so be saved. For this reason God sends them a powerful delusion so that they will believe the lie and so that all will be condemned who have not believed the truth but have delighted in wickedness. (2 Thessalonians 2:9-12)

CHAPTER 4

NATURAL DISASTERS AND SIGNS FROM HEAVEN

There will be great earthquakes, famines and pestilences in various places, and fearful events and great signs from heaven. (Luke 21:11, quoting Jesus)

All these are the beginning of birth pains. (Matthew 24:8, quoting Jesus)

There will be signs in the sun, moon and stars. On the earth, nations will be in anguish and perplexity at the roaring and tossing of the sea. Men will faint from terror, apprehensive of what is coming on the world, for the heavenly bodies will be shaken. (Luke 21:25-26, quoting Jesus)

I watched as he opened the sixth seal. There was a great earthquake. The sun turned black like sackcloth made of goat hair, the whole moon turned blood red, and the stars in the sky fell to earth, as late figs drop from a fig tree when shaken by a strong wind. The sky receded like a scroll, rolling up, and every mountain and island was removed from its place. (Revelation 6:12-14)

His eyes are like blazing fire, and on his head are many crowns. He has a name written on him that no one knows but he himself. He is dressed in a robe dipped in blood, and his name is the Word of God. The armies of heaven were following him, riding on white horses and dressed in fine linen, white and clean. Out of his mouth comes a sharp sword with which to strike down the nations. "He will rule them with an iron scepter." He treads the winepress of the fury of the wrath of God Almighty. On his robe and on his thigh he has this name written: KING OF KINGS AND LORD OF LORDS. (Revelation 19:12-16)

CHAPTER 5

THE MORAL DECAY OF SOCIETY

But mark this: There will be terrible times in the last days. People will be lovers of themselves, lovers of money, boastful, proud, abusive, disobedient to their parents, ungrateful, unholy, without love, unforgiving, slanderous, without self-control, brutal, not lovers of the good, treacherous, rash, conceited, lovers of pleasure rather than lovers of God. (2 Timothy 3:1-4)

Therefore God gave them over in the sinful desires of their hearts to sexual impurity for the degrading of their bodies with one another.

They exchanged the truth of God for a lie, and worshiped and served created things rather than the Creator—who is forever praised. Amen. Because of this, God gave them over to shameful lusts. Even their women exchanged natural relations for unnatural ones. In the same way the men also abandoned natural relations with women and were inflamed with lust for one another. Men committed indecent acts with other men, and received in themselves the due penalty for their perversion. (Romans 1:26-27)

Do you not know that the wicked will not inherit the kingdom of God? Do not be deceived: Neither the sexually immoral nor idolaters nor adulterers nor male prostitutes nor homosexual offenders nor thieves nor the greedy nor drunkards nor slanderers nor swindlers will inherit the kingdom of God. (1 Corinthians 6:9-10)

CHAPTER 6

INCREASE OF APOSTASY IN THE CHURCH

At that time many will turn away from the faith and will betray and hate each other, and many false prophets will appear and deceive many people. (Matthew 24:10-11, quoting Jesus)

For the time will come when men will not put up with sound doctrine. Instead, to suit their own desires, they will gather around them a great number of teachers to say what their itching ears want to hear. They will turn their ears away from the truth and turn aside to myths. (2 Timothy 4:3-4)

Christ praises the churches that do not tolerate wicked persons (2:2); that test the doctrinal viewpoints, behavior, and claims made by Christian leaders (2:2); that persevere in hardship, suffering, faithfulness, love, witness, service and suffering for Christ

(2:3,10,13,19,26); that hate that which God hates (2:6); that overcomes sin, Satan and the ungodly world (2:7,11,17,26; 3:5,12,21); that refuse to conform to immorality in the world and worldliness in the church (2:24; 3:4); and that obeys God's Word (3:8,10)

We all stumble in many ways. (James 3:2)

So, if you think you are standing firm, be careful that you don't fall! No temptation has seized you except what is common to man. And God is faithful; he will not let you be tempted beyond what you can bear. But when you are tempted, he will also provide a way out so that you can stand up under it. (1 Corinthians 10:12-13)

So I find this law at work: When I want to do good, evil is right there with me. For in my inner being I delight in God's law; but I see another law at work in the members of my body, waging war against the law of my mind and making me a prisoner of the law of sin at work within my members. What a wretched man I am! Who will rescue me from this body of death? Thanks be to God— through Jesus Christ our Lord! So then, I myself in my mind am a slave to God's law, but in the sinful nature a slave to the law of sin. (Romans 7:21-24)

If we deliberately keep on sinning after we have received the knowledge of the truth, no sacrifice for sins is left, but only a fearful expectation of judgment and of raging fire that will consume the enemies of God. Anyone who rejected the law of Moses died without mercy on the testimony of two or three witnesses. How much more severely do you think a man deserves to be punished who has trampled the Son of God under foot, who has treated as an unholy thing the blood of the covenant that sanctified him, and who has insulted the Spirit of grace? (Hebrews 10:26-29)

The acts of the sinful nature are obvious: sexual immorality, impurity and debauchery; idolatry and witchcraft; hatred, discord, jealousy, fits of rage, selfish ambition, dissensions, factions and envy; drunkenness, orgies, and the like. I warn you, as I did before, that those who live like this will not inherit the kingdom of God. (Galatians 5:19-20)

If any one of you is without sin, let him be the first to throw a stone. (John 8:7, quoting Jesus)

Go now and leave your life of sin. (John 8:11, quoting Jesus)

For all have sinned and fall short of the glory of God. (Romans 3:23)

Do we, then, nullify the law by this faith? Not at all! Rather, we uphold the law. (Romans 3:31)

Dear children, do not let anyone lead you astray. He who does what is right is righteous, just as he is righteous. He who does what is sinful is of the devil, because the devil has been sinning from the beginning. The reason the Son of God appeared was to destroy the devil's work. No one who is born of God will continue to sin, because God's seed remains in him; he cannot go on sinning, because he has been born of God. This is how we know who the children of God are and who the children of the devil are: Anyone who does not do what is right is not a child of God; nor is anyone who does not love his brother. (1 John 3:7-11)

"Not everyone who says to Me, 'Lord, Lord,' shall enter the kingdom of heaven, but he who does the will of My Father in heaven. Many will say to Me in that day, 'Lord, Lord, have we not prophesied in Your name, cast out demons in Your name, and done many wonders in Your name?' And then I will declare to them, 'I never knew you; depart from Me, you who practice lawlessness!' (Matthew 7:21-23, quoting Jesus)

But you know that he appeared so that he might take away our sins. And in him is no sin. No one who lives in him keeps on sinning. No one who continues to sin has either seen him or known him. (1 John 3:5-6)

"Enter through the narrow gate. For wide is the gate and broad is the road that leads to destruction, and many enter through it. But small is the gate and narrow the road that leads to life, and only a few find it." (Matthew 7:13-14, quoting Jesus)

For the grace of God that brings salvation has appeared to all men. It teaches us to say "No" to ungodliness and worldly passions, and to live self-controlled, upright and godly lives in this present age, while we wait for the blessed hope—the glorious appearing of our great God and Savior, Jesus Christ, who gave himself for us to redeem us from all wickedness and to purify for himself a people that are his very own, eager to do what is good. (Titus 2:11-14)

Now, brothers, I know that you acted in ignorance, as did your leaders. But this is how God fulfilled what he had foretold through all the prophets, saying that his Christ would suffer. Repent, then, and turn to God, so that your sins may be wiped out. (Acts 3:13)

CHAPTER 7

CURRENT WORLD POLITICS AND BIBLE PROPHECY

The word of the LORD came to me: "Son of man, set your face against Gog, of the land of Magog, the chief prince of Meshech and Tubal; prophesy against him and say: 'This is what the Sovereign LORD says: I am against you, O Gog, chief prince of Meshech and Tubal. I will turn you around, put hooks in your jaws and bring you out with your whole army—your horses, your horsemen fully armed, and a great horde with large and small shields, all of them brandishing their swords. Persia, Cush and Put will be with them, all with shields and helmets, also Gomer with all its troops, and Beth Togarmah from the far north with all its troops—the many nations with you. (Ezekiel 38:1-6)

You will say, "I will invade a land of unwalled villages; I will attack a peaceful and unsuspecting people—all of them living without walls and without gates and bars. I will plunder and loot and turn my hand against the resettled ruins and the people gathered from the nations, rich in livestock and goods, living at the center of the land." (Ezekiel 38:11-12)

"You looked, O king, and there before you stood a large statue—an enormous, dazzling statue, awesome in appearance. The head of the statue was made of pure gold, its chest and arms of silver, its belly and thighs of bronze, its legs of iron, its feet partly of iron and partly of baked clay." (Daniel 2:31-33)

You will hear of wars and rumors of wars, but see to it that you are not alarmed. Such things must happen, but the end is still to come. (Matthew 24:6, quoting Jesus)

CHAPTER 8

THE UNITED STATES' ROLE IN END-TIMES PROPHECY

I am going to make Jerusalem a cup that sends all the surrounding peoples reeling. Judah will be besieged as well as Jerusalem. On that day, when all the nations of the earth are gathered against her, I will make Jerusalem an immovable rock for all the nations. All who try to move it will injure themselves. (Zechariah 12:2-3)

When the Lamb opened the third seal, I heard the third living creature say, "Come!" I looked, and there before me was a black horse! Its rider was holding a pair of scales in his hand. Then I heard what sounded like a voice among the four living creatures, saying, "A quart of wheat for a day's wages, and three quarts of barley for a day's wages, and do not damage the oil and the wine! (Revelation 6:5-6)

He also forced everyone, small and great, rich and poor, free and slave, to receive a mark on his right hand or on his forehead, so that no one could buy or sell unless he had the mark, which is the name of the beast or the number of his name. This calls for wisdom. If anyone has insight, let him calculate the number of the beast, for it is man's number. His number is 666. (Revelation 13:16-18.)

CHAPTER 9

TECHNOLOGY ENABLES END-TIMES EVENTS

For three and a half days men from every people, tribe, language and nation will gaze on their bodies and refuse them burial. (Revelation 11:9)

And this gospel of the kingdom will be preached in the whole world as a testimony to all nations, and then the end will come. (Matthew 24:12, quoting Jesus)

A third angel followed them and said in a loud voice: "If anyone worships the beast and his image and receives his mark on the forehead or on the hand, he, too, will drink of the wine of God's fury, which has been poured full strength into the cup of his wrath. He will be tormented with burning sulfur in the presence of the holy angels and of the Lamb. And the smoke of their torment rises for ever and ever. There is no rest day or night for those who worship the beast and his image, or for anyone who receives the mark of his name." (Revelation 14:9-11)

And I saw what looked like a sea of glass mixed with fire and, standing beside the sea, those who had been victorious over the beast and his image and over the number of his name. They held harps given them by God. (Revelation 15:2)

The first angel went and poured out his bowl on the land, and ugly and painful sores broke out on the people who had the mark of the beast and worshiped his image. (Revelation 16:2)

But the beast was captured, and with him the false prophet who had performed the miraculous signs on his behalf. With these signs he had deluded those who had received the mark of the beast and worshiped his image. The two of them were thrown alive into the fiery lake of burning sulfur. (Revelation 19:20)

I saw thrones on which were seated those who had been given authority to judge. And I saw the souls of those who had been beheaded because of their testimony for Jesus and because of the word of God. They had not worshiped the beast or his image and had not received his mark on their foreheads or their hands. They came to life and reigned with Christ a thousand years. (Revelation 20:4)

CHAPTER 10

SIGNS TO WATCH FOR

The sixth angel poured out his bowl on the great river Euphrates, and its water was dried up to prepare the way for the kings of the East. (Revelation 16:12)

When the Lamb opened the fourth seal, I heard the voice of the fourth living creature say, "Come!" I looked, and there before me was a pale horse! Its rider was named Death, and Hades was following close behind him. They were given power over a fourth of the earth to kill by sword, famine and plague, and by the wild beasts of the earth. (Revelation 6:7-8)

CHAPTER 11

FURTHER STUDY

A great and wondrous sign appeared in heaven: a woman clothed with the sun, with the moon under her feet and a crown of twelve stars on her head. She was pregnant and cried out in pain as she was about to give birth. (Revelation 12:1-2)

MESSIANIC PROPHECY

Jesus would be born in the town of Bethlehem

Old Testament Prophecy: "But you, Bethlehem, though you are small among the clans of Judah, out of you will come for me one who will be ruler over Israel." (Micah 5:2)

New Testament Fulfillment: "After Jesus was born in Bethlehem ..." (Matthew 2:1)

Jesus would have His hands and feet pierced

Old Testament Prophecy: "The assembly of the wicked have enclosed me. They have pierced my hands and my feet." (Psalm 22:16)

New Testament Fulfillment: "And when they came to the place, which is called Calvary, there they crucified him and the criminals, one on the right and the other on the left." (Luke 23:33)

Jesus would be sold for thirty pieces of silver

Old Testament Prophecy: "So they weighed out thirty pieces of silver for my price." (Zechariah 11:12)

New Testament Fulfillment: "And they agreed with him for thirty pieces of silver." (Matthew 26:15)

Lots would be cast for Jesus' clothing

Old Testament Prophecy: "They divide my garments among them, and for my clothing they cast lots." (Psalm 22:18)

New Testament Fulfillment: "And when they had crucified Him, they divided up His garments among themselves by casting lots." (Matthew 27:35)

CHAPTER 12

WHAT TO DO NOW

At that time Michael, the great prince who protects your people, will arise. There will be a time of distress such as has not happened from the beginning of nations until then. But at that time your people—everyone whose name is found written in the book—will be delivered. Multitudes who sleep in the dust of the earth will awake: some to everlasting life, others to shame and everlasting contempt. Those who are wise will shine like the brightness of the heavens, and those who lead many to righteousness, like the stars for ever and ever. But you, Daniel, close up and seal the words of the scroll until the time of the end. Many will go here and there to increase knowledge. (Daniel 12:1-4)

If any of you lacks wisdom, he should ask God, who gives generously to all without finding fault, and it will be given to him. But when he asks, he must believe and not doubt, because he who doubts is like a wave of the sea, blown and tossed by the wind. (James 1:5-6)

Now, brothers, about times and dates we do not need to write to you, for you know very well that the day of the Lord will come like a thief in the night. While people are saying, "Peace and safety," destruction will come on them suddenly, as labor pains on a pregnant woman, and they will not escape. But you, brothers, are not in darkness so that this day should surprise you like a thief. You are all sons of the light and sons of the day. We do not belong to the night or to the darkness. So then, let us not be like others, who are asleep, but let us be alert and self-controlled. For those who sleep, sleep at night, and those who get drunk, get drunk at night. But since we belong to the day, let us be self-controlled, putting on faith and love as a breastplate, and the hope of salvation as a helmet. For God did not appoint us to suffer wrath but to receive salvation through our Lord Jesus Christ. He died for us so that, whether we are awake or asleep, we may live together with him. Therefore encourage one another and build each other up, just as in fact you are doing. (Thessalonians 5:1-9)

Let us not give up meeting together, as some are in the habit of doing, but let us encourage one another—and all the more as you see the Day approaching. (Hebrews 10:25)

Just as it was in the days of Noah, so also will it be in the days of the Son of Man. People were eating, drinking, marrying and being given in marriage up to the day Noah entered the ark. Then the flood came and destroyed them all. It was the same in the days of Lot. People were eating and drinking, buying and selling, planting and building. But the day Lot left Sodom, fire and sulfur rained down from heaven and destroyed them all. It will be just like this on the day the Son of Man is revealed. On that day no one who is on the roof of his house, with his goods inside, should go down to get them. Likewise, no one in the field should go back for anything. Remember Lot's wife! Whoever tries to keep his life will lose it, and whoever loses his life will preserve it. I tell you, on that night two people will be in one bed; one will be taken and the other left. Two women will be grinding grain together; one will be taken and the other left. Two men will be in a field; one taken, the other left. (Luke 17:26-36)

How To Become A Christian

"Here I am! I stand at the door and knock. If anyone hears my voice and opens the door, I will come in and eat with him, and he with me." (Revelation 3:20, quoting Jesus)

I tell you the truth, no one can see the kingdom of God unless he is born again. (John 3:3, quoting Jesus)

You shall have no other gods before me. (Exodus 20:3)

I am the way and the truth and the life. No one comes to the Father except through me. (John 14:6, quoting Jesus)

For all have sinned, and fall short of the glory of God. (Romans 3:23)

If we claim to be without sin, we deceive ourselves and the truth is not in us. If we confess our sins, he is faithful and just and will forgive us our sins and purify us from all unrighteousness. (1 John 1:8-9)

For God so loved the world that he gave his one and only Son, that whoever believes in him shall not perish but have eternal life. For God did not send his Son into the world to condemn the world, but to save the world through him. (John 3:16-17)

Therefore, I urge you, brothers, in view of God's mercy, to offer your bodies as living sacrifices, holy and pleasing to God—this is your spiritual act of worship. Do not conform any longer to the pattern of this world, but be transformed by the renewing of your mind. Then you will be able to test and approve what God's will is—his good, pleasing and perfect will. (Romans 12:1-2)

ADDITIONAL RESOURCES

Web Site
The *Learn Bible Prophecy Ministries'* web site keeps a list of valuable, biblically-sound resources to help you better learn Bible prophecy.

www.LearnBibleProphecy.com

Prophecy News
The following web page has a list of current headlines related to Bible prophecy:

www.LearnBibleProphecy.com/**news**

Facebook
If you would like to conveniently get relevant prophecy-related updates posted on your Facebook news feeds a few times a week, visit our Facebook page and then "Like" it.

www.LearnBibleProphecy.com/**facebook**

Made in the USA
Charleston, SC
08 October 2014